START Here ↓

TEACHING & LEARNING WITH ADULTS

Barbara Bruce

DISCIPLESHIP RESOURCES

P.O. BOX 340003 • NASHVILLE, TN 37203-0003
www.discipleshipresources.org

Cover design by Sharon Anderson

Book design by Nanci H. Lamar

Edited by Debra D. Smith and Heidi L. Hewitt

ISBN 0-88177-303-4

Library of Congress Catalog Card No. 99-65956

DR303

Contents

Preface

This book comes out of a love for working with adults and a realization that doing what we have always done, only harder, does not give us better results.

We are at an amazing time and place in the history of our planet. We are privileged to be on the cusp of the most exciting time ever. God is calling us to make disciples. What an awesome challenge lies before us. God is calling us to a ministry of change, of service, of love.

In my years of researching and working with adults, I have made several observations: Adults are fun. Adults are eager to learn. Adults are searching for meaning. Adults are willing, if a bit reluctant at first, to experiment and play with their own learning. Adults often are amazed at their own insights when given permission to express themselves in different ways. Adults want to know more about the Bible.

The task of teaching adults may seem overwhelming. How can you possibly do all those things? Teaching and learning with adults is a multifaceted process. Many things are happening at once. This book will help you address issues of which you may or may not have been consciously aware. You will find the same information in several places and contexts. One of the edicts of learning is repetition, repetition, repetition. The more ways you can connect concepts, the more you will learn them.

You do not have to do everything at once. Some concepts may seem new or unfamiliar. Try things in small steps and test the waters for yourself and for your adult students.

This book helps teachers and leaders of adults to see the big picture, to explore the many and varied options for teaching and learning. It gives insights into how adults learn and grow in faith and introduces some adults and their specific needs. It asks probing questions for making disciples.

This book is an invitation to make discoveries and find delight in working with adults, as I have. It is a gift of love.

Barbara Bruce

Introduction

What Is an Adult?

When did you first know you were an adult?
- When you attained full size and strength?
- When you voted for the first time?
- When your car insurance rates began to decline?
- When you were called sir or ma'am for the first time?
- When you walked across a stage and received a diploma?
- When you began to recognize the songs on the oldies station?
- When you applied for your first mortgage?
- When your vehicle of choice had four doors?
- When a long-term commitment was more than a day and a half?

What is an adult? It is a difficult question to answer. For some, adulthood is reaching a specific age. For others, adulthood comes on quickly when responsibility must be shouldered. For some, adulthood is to be avoided as long as possible. For others, it is reaching a new and exciting stage of life.

I believe being adult is an attitude. Being adult is putting away childish things and taking on the responsibility that goes along with making decisions and commitments. Being adult is recognizing that you do not know it all, that life is a journey, that faith is active, that there are more than six billion people in the world who do not know who you are but that God does.

Using This Book

How does the church meet the diverse needs of adults? How can we minister to adults? What can the church do to be true to its mission of accepting, teaching, nurturing, and sending forth people to live in the world as disciples? These are monumental questions, and I do not claim to have the answers. However, there are many right answers—many ways the church, your church, can help adults find God in their lives and share God with others.

This book consists of three parts: "What?" "So What?" and "Now What?" "What?" provides information on some of the latest research related to how adults learn. "So What?" looks at how the information on adult learning applies to everyday lives and introduces you to real people, their stories and their needs. These people are not unique, for every church has people in similar circumstances. I encourage you to read about them and discover how their stories can help you understand the adults you work with. "Now What?" challenges you to look at what lies ahead in the future of adult education. Some things we know; other things we can only guess at.

I invite you to work within (or beyond) the framework of this book and find answers that fit your situation. Join me on this journey. Make notes in the margins and blank spaces. This book is designed as an interactive resource. I have done my part. Now you need to do yours by responding to the questions, finding people in similar circumstances in your church, and working on the issues.

Begin with the pretest on the next page. It will help you to identify your existing assumptions and understandings about how adults learn. After you have worked through this book with your adults students, take the posttest (page 83) to see if your attitudes and understandings have changed.

Take the information presented and make it yours. Have fun with it. Learn from it and with it. Adapt it. Turn it around and use it in ways that help you to help others in your church and beyond. Wrestle with the issues raised; then decide what might work in your class, in your church.

Pretest

Write an *A* for *Agree*, a *D* for *Disagree*, or a *U* for *Undecided* beside each statement.

___ 1. The major ministry with adults is to encourage memorizing Scripture to use in times of need.

___ 2. Adults learn in a variety of ways.

___ 3. Adults need a safe environment in order to speak what is on their hearts.

___ 4. Community building is a waste of precious time with people who attend church together.

___ 5. Adults go through predictable transitions of faith development throughout their lives.

___ 6. Adult classes need to be pastor-led to have credibility.

___ 7. Adults need a structured class setting in order to learn.

___ 8. Expression of feelings has no place in an adult class.

___ 9. Many adults are searching for a meaningful faith.

___ 10. Adult classes must meet on Sunday morning to have the most impact on people's lives.

___ 11. Adults come to class with many and diverse wants and needs.

___ 12. Every adult class must have a trained teacher to be effective.

___ 13. Storytelling is for children.

___ 14. Prayer is a vital part of any adult Christian learning situation.

___ 15. Every adult class needs to stick with the chosen curriculum for the best learning to happen.

___ 16. Many adults are embarrassed by their lack of biblical knowledge.

___ 17. The Coffeepot Class (just hanging out) is an excuse for adults who do not want to learn.

___ 18. Adult classes work best when they are homogeneous in nature.

___ 19. You must have a minimum of ten adults for a class to be successful.

Section One
What?

How Do Adults Learn?

- Adults learn in many ways.
- Adults learn what they want to learn, what they are interested in.
- Adults link new information to what they already know.
- Adults learn when they believe they can use the new information.
- Adults learn when they are comfortable and feel safe.

Educational theory tells us only what the latest research has discovered about how people learn. It is up to us to test it and experiment with it in our own teaching and learning situations. In this section, you will learn about some of the more recent theories about how people learn and how you can use the methods developed from these theories to become a more effective teacher of adults.

Brain Research

The human brain consists of billions of cells and is one of the most complex objects in the known universe. Is it any wonder, then, that people have been fascinated with the brain for thousands of years? Some people who have been associated with early brain research are Aristotle, Plato, and da Vinci. The earliest study was based on fascination with how the brain functions. Without technology, it was difficult to go much further than observation and educated guess. About fifty years ago, interest was generated again in discovering more about this roughly three pounds of tissue that is the center of our being.

In the recent past, brain research consisted of stimulus and response. Behavior could be programmed by punishing or rewarding animals as they learned such things as finding their way through a maze. Unfortunately, some educational systems never moved beyond that theory and still metaphorically reward students for right answers (*A's*) and punish for wrong answers (*F's*).

Brain research in humans followed as victims of strokes were studied. Researchers discovered that the human brain has two hemispheres, with each controlling a different side of the body and different functions. Research is continuing to provide answers about what happens in each of the brain hemispheres.

Through the wonder of brain imaging technology, we actually can see where things are happening in the brain. These things are not happening the same for all people, because an individual's circumstances determine in which hemisphere reading, writing, music, and all of the abilities function best. What we, as educators, are doing is building on this continuing research in how we think and learn. Many brain researchers now take a holistic approach and contend that research is changing our understanding so rapidly that one can hardly keep up.

The mind-body connection has regenerated much interest in the last few decades. Mental imaging may appear to be a relatively new field, but Chinese culture has used this belief in mind-body connection in the practice of medicine for thousand of years. The Bible speaks of this connection in the wisdom literature: "A tranquil mind gives life to the flesh, but passion makes the bones rot" (Proverbs 14:30). Physicians and educators are constantly working to discover more information to make the mind-body connection work to heal and to increase our ability to learn.

In the past ten years, more research has been done on the brain than in all the previous history combined. With the use of scans—CAT (computerized axial tomography), MRI (magnetic resonance imaging), and PET (positron emission tomography)—physicians and scientists are able to see the functioning of the brain.

So what does brain research have to do with teaching and learning with adults? Physicians and scientists are not the only people who are interested in the brain. Educators are taking this information and applying it to how people learn.

We still have much to learn about how the brain works and what the implications of this are for adult learning. However, knowledge of what is being learned from both the behavioral sciences and brain studies can help you design opportunities to enhance the learning of the adults you teach. For example, for most people intrinsic (internal) motivation is stronger than extrinsic (external) motivation in directing long-term learning. Some research suggests that learning is stimulated not by praise and punishment but by our inner want and need to learn. Adults learn what they want to learn.

All adults do not learn in the same way. Some adults crave structure and learn in a linear path. Others learn in circular or spiral paths, making connections through different senses and relationships.

As in all of life, balance is the key. The best and most-comprehensive learning occurs when we are engaged in a variety of ways with the content being presented. The more senses we use in learning, the more places in our brain the information can be stored. Think of it as a computer file. If you want to retrieve information and ensure its safe keeping, file it under different names and in different places. Using many senses helps us to retrieve information in several ways—through sight, sound, taste, touch, and smell. All of our senses connect learning and stimulate thinking.

At one time it was believed that our brains were fully developed at birth and that we lost huge numbers of brain cells as we grew older. Mental decline was thought to be a normal part of aging. Current research indicates that just as physical exercise is important for maintaining our physical health, mental exercise is important for maintaining mental health. It appears that challenging mental activity actually strengthens the connections in our brain cells. We can assume that the longer we are engaged in learning new and challenging information, the more we continue to keep our brains functioning at maximum levels. The basic use-it-or-lose-it axiom of physical exercise applies to mental exercise as well.

We must continue to challenge adults to keep thinking. In Hebrews it is clearly stated that we, as people who want to continue to increase our faith, must go beyond simply feeding milk to adults: "But solid food is for the mature, for those whose faculties have been trained by practice to distinguish good from evil" (Hebrews 5:14). We must encourage adults to think, question, and make connections.

We must provide for emotional as well as intellectual experience. All learning happens in the presence of some form of emotional energy. Good learning includes and encourages the expression of emotions. When emotions are engaged, learning is more profound, occurs at a deeper level, and is retained for a longer period of time.

To function optimally, we must switch gears from time to time. Change the pace of the class about every twenty minutes to stimulate thinking. You need not change topic, but move from giving information, to having reflection time, to having discussion, to writing. Changing the pace keeps the learning fresh and stimulating. Even changing physical positions helps alter perspective.

12 Tips for Teaching

1. Create a positive learning environment by establishing and maintaining ground rules.
2. Engage emotions in learning.
3. Connect learning with life experience.
4. Encourage learners to focus and concentrate.
5. Reinforce learning by using a variety of methods that appeal to different ways of learning.
6. Use humor (but never in a way that belittles or puts down).
7. Change the pace about every twenty minutes.
8. Create opportunities for physical movement.
9. Encourage participants to reflect on what they are learning and experiencing.
10. Allow self-discovery to create owned learning.
11. Be succinct. More is not always better.
12. Summarize learning as the class ends, and begin the next class session by reflecting on previous learning.

Learning Hooks

Learning hooks, or preteaching strategies, assist students by presenting something that will help them assimilate information. New learning is based on old learning; therefore, we need a process to trigger our memory of things we already know so that we can build on them.

Effective learning hooks, which are not difficult to do, greatly enhance student learning. Once you see the results and get into the habit of using them, you will wonder how you taught without them. Learning hooks require an active and explicit approach by the teacher in order to be useful.

Incorporate as many learning hooks as appropriate in each lesson to help ground and focus the learning. Learning hooks may be used at the beginning, middle, or end of the lesson, depending on your goal. Vary the learning hooks, and inform your students of what you are doing and why. Once students become aware of how much their learning is deepened, they will include the learning hooks themselves. Never assume anything about what adults already know about the Bible or other faith-related issues. Experiment with any combination of the following hooks and watch your adult learners' interest and understanding deepen.

Find Common Ground

Try to find an area of mutual experience for the class to relate to as a way to provide a foundation for your lesson. If you are dealing with the story of the good Samaritan, ask when they have been robbed (if not literally, then metaphorically robbed of time or dignity), when they have passed by someone who needed help, when they have stopped to help someone in need.

If you are dealing with the story of Ruth, ask if anyone has moved and left behind all that is familiar. Ask how it feels to be in a new place. In a new place, you do not know where to find a good doctor or baby sitter. Everything is strange, and it takes time to get to know your surroundings and establish a comfort level again.

Shared experiences help adult students to level the playing field. Everyone has had, or knows someone who has had, a similar experience. Discussing personal and relevant experiences will help to anchor your lesson and make it live for the students.

Use Questions

Asking questions will help your adult students connect to the lesson what they already know and will enhance learning. Ask: "Why, do you think, did the priest and Levite not stop to help the man who had been beaten up by robbers?" or "We know that the Pharisees were continually trying to trap Jesus. What, do you think, was their motive in bringing the adulterous woman to Jesus before stoning her?" Questions that help people make connections are critical to adult learning. To give the lesson greater impact, ask questions that will help your adult students connect known information or make educated guesses.

Draw On Prior Knowledge

Seldom do we go into a situation without prior knowledge. Usually, we have information we may not be aware we have. Using methods to activate adults' memory of what they already know will help to link new information to old. Using a statement such as "Tell me everything you know about..." and recording the answers on newsprint or on a chalkboard will help adult students realize that they do know something about the topic. Be sure to record all answers, even those you know are incorrect. When you have finished your lesson, look at the answers the students gave earlier to see what was right and what was not. Be sure to tell your adult students that this is an indication of how we connect information. It also is a measure of how much all of us have to learn about our biblical heritage.

Expose Misconceptions

Recording misinformation is an important piece of the mix. When I recently asked an adult class to tell me all they knew about the good Samaritan, a student replied, "The Samaritan woman went to the well." I wrote this information down along with all the other information that was provided. As the person who gave me that piece of information listened to everything else that was said, he made the connection and realized he was thinking of another story. He learned the difference. What is important here is that he learned.

Misconceptions block new learning. We cannot connect new information when what we already have is wrong. Things will not make sense, students will become frustrated, and learning will shut down. Often, the misconceptions are buried, and then confusion grows. Try to find ways to uncover misconceptions about words, terms, characters, and stories. Once the misconception has been corrected, connections can be made to new learning.

Explain at the beginning of class that everyone comes with some misconceptions and lack of understanding. Then assure them that it is all right. Most adult learners will be relieved to hear that. Tell them that everyone in the class, including the teacher, is there to learn and grow in faith through increasing his or her understanding.

Clarify Vocabulary

Vocabulary is crucial to understanding, so make sure your adult students understand the words and how they are used in the lesson. For example, make sure they know what a priest and a Levite were. Their roles in the parable of the good Samaritan add meaning to the story. They have been presented as the bad guys in this story, but they were living the letter of the law. Make sure your students know who Samaritans were and that Samaritans and Jews disliked one another because of religious beliefs. This clarification of vocabulary adds a depth of understanding to the story that is lacking without it. The Samaritan was living the spirit of the law by acting out of compassion for the abused traveler.

Keep a good Bible dictionary in the classroom and have the class look at vocabulary every week. This will take away any discomfort they feel about not knowing the meanings of words. Show them by example that they need to understand vocabulary.

Create Interest

Be creative in your presentation of material. You might bring in a box of random items and ask your adult students to choose an item and talk with someone else in the class about how that item is like your lesson theme. This way of beginning the lesson will help to get students talking and thinking about the topic and set the stage for deeper learning.

Reading a poem, bringing in an object, showing a picture, and playing music are all are ways of stimulating interest in the lesson. This method helps students to get focused on the topic of the lesson. They are then already involved.

Connect Learning to Life

Help adult students see how what they learn in your class reaches beyond the church setting and into their lives. Information is learned better and has a more-lasting impression when they can apply it to their daily living. Make sure each lesson connects with their lives at home, at work, and in informal settings such as sports events and community service projects.

This linking to real life will prove to be a great factor in how adult students approach the lesson. Linking can be as simple as asking how they might apply the message of today's Scripture to their lives. Ask if they know of situations being lived out today that are like the one in the lesson. Then ask how they might behave differently after today's lesson.

Some Things to Think About

1. Review the "12 Tips for Teaching" (page 12). Which have you experienced as a teacher or learner, and how did they affect learning?

2. Which of the tips do you already incorporate in your learning? Decide on two or three to use intentionally in your next class. Then gradually increase the number you use.

3. Think of a class you have led recently or intend to lead. List a way you could use each of the learning hooks.

   • Find common ground

   • Use questions

   • Draw on prior knowledge

   • Expose misconceptions

   • Clarify vocabulary

   • Create interest

   • Connect learning to life

4. How will you determine which hooks work best for each lesson?

Components of a Lesson

Just as this book is constructed of three major components—"What?" "So What?" and "Now What?"—a good lesson also has three major components.

The first component ("What?") focuses on information. This is the place where the learning hooks are critical. When adult students can make connections through previous knowledge, vocabulary, and background information, a wonderful foundation for new learning takes place. We sometimes neglect this component when doing Bible study, because we assume that adults have biblical knowledge. This is not always an accurate assumption. For example, knowing that many Jews considered the Samaritans as inferior adds a new depth of understanding to the story of the good Samaritan. Bible dictionaries and commentaries are invaluable resources for gathering information. Adult learners cannot make leaps of understanding without the foundational components. They must get a basic understanding of the background, in order to make connections for their own learning.

The second component ("So What?") is the part of the lesson where the student asks questions such as, "How can I connect this information with my life? What is it in this story that speaks to me?" If there is no connection with real life, then it is just a story. I do not believe there is much in the Bible that does not connect with who we are today, for it is a book about God's relationship with humankind. Whatever we experience has been experienced in some way by our predecessors. The "So What?" segment is important because it helps us to see that we have been—and are still—a people in a relationship with our God.

We all can relate to biblical characters who found excuses not to follow God's instructions. We all have denied Jesus in some way (by action or inaction). We all have held the stone of condemnation and judgment. Asking questions that connect God's story with our story makes the Bible live and take on critical meaning for our lives today. The biblical story leaps from the page and touches our hearts and minds. The Bible is so exciting because it is a living document.

The third component ("Now What?") is the part that makes the lesson faith forming and transforming. This is the part that asks, "Now that I know this information and can connect it with my life, what will I do differently? How will my life be changed?" These are faith questions that bring God's message home and have the potential to be life changing. When we fail to ask the "Now What?" questions, we miss the opportunity to make learning formational as well as informational.

Some Things to Think About

Think about the classes in which you participate, either as a teacher or as a student. Are all three parts of the lesson present? Does a particular part need to be emphasized more?

For each of the sections of the lesson, list three ways you might lead that section.

What?

1.

2.

3.

So What?

1.

2.

3.

Now What?

1.

2.

3.

Multiple Intelligences

One of the most significant advances in education has come through the work of Dr. Howard Gardner of Harvard University. His theory of multiple intelligences has important implications for those who lead classes of adult learners. Briefly stated, Gardner believes that the traditional method of measuring intelligence, the IQ test, actually measures only certain types of intelligence. He theorizes that a variety of intelligences influence the ways people learn. In his book *Frames of Mind: The Theory of Multiple Intelligences* (Basic Books, 1983), Gardner identifies a number of particular intelligences. Research continues to discover others. (The various types will be discussed later.)

Although each of us has the capacity to learn using all of the different intelligences, most of us have certain intelligences that are more effective for us. Most adult educators in Western cultures use perhaps three or four of the intelligences in their teaching. The result is that people whose preferred ways of learning are not included often drop out or choose not to participate in learning experiences.

As teachers and leaders of adults, we must be aware of the different types of intelligences and strive to incorporate as many of them in our lessons as possible. This is not as difficult as it may appear, for we may unconsciously be using some of them already. Listed below is a brief description of each intelligence and suggested ways to awaken and activate that intelligence in your lessons. You will see that one activity may incorporate several intelligences. In my experience, intelligences rarely stand alone. To complete many of the tasks of daily living, we must use the intelligences in combination with one another. The various intelligences build on one another to enhance and enrich learning.

Learning Through Written or Spoken Word (Verbal/Linguistic)

Language shapes our understanding of our world. Words can excite, inspire, entertain, enlighten, or depress us. The power of words—whether read, heard, written, or spoken—can bring about profound changes in our lives.

Think of words of Scripture that speak profoundly to you, and ask yourself why those particular words affect you. For many, the poetry and beauty of the Psalms speak of peace and renew faith. In times of crisis, words of Scripture may bring reassurance and calm. People who learn best through written or spoken word love to read and write. They like knowing the derivation and precise meaning of words. In addition, verbal/linguistic learners have a sensitivity to flow and order of words and understand the different functions of language. They express themselves well in both the written and spoken language and like to play with words, do crossword puzzles, and read and write prose and poetry. They often are fascinated with other languages and love the play on words of puns. I have observed that people who have a strong preference for using this intelligence often choose careers or pleasure as authors, editors, journalists, TV or radio reporters, and speech writers.

To encourage the use of this intelligence with adults, do the following:

- Read Scripture in several different translations, such as the King James Version, New International Version, New Revised Standard Version, Contemporary English Version.
- Ask which translation and which words help learners understand and apply the story to their own lives.
- List vocabulary words that may not be clear. Then explain the words and ask how understanding them adds meaning to the story.
- Invite the learners to tell the story in their own words or to rewrite the story in contemporary terms.
- Have the class break into groups of twos or threes and discuss what the story means to them.
- Ask the learners to record insights from the lesson in a journal or reflection log.
- Have the learners write a poem about the lesson or about insights gained from the lesson.
- Have the learners debate an issue. Give them opposite sides of a topic to defend (such as "Being a Christian affects decisions I make in my job" versus "Being a Christian does not affect decisions I make in my job").
- Use poetry and stories to present information.

Cognitive and Rational Learning (Logical-Mathematical)

People who learn best in a logical-mathematical way are motivated by finding relationships between ideas. They tend to think in numbers and abstract symbols and are able to see patterns and put together chains of ideas.

People who prefer learning in this way like an outline, a logical reason for what they do, information, and statistics. They enjoy using facts, statistics, research, comparisons, problem solving, mathematical equations, distances and maps. To fully engage the logical-mathematical learner, include facts, logical sequences, and deductions. They function best when their world is orderly, precise, logical, and pragmatic. I have observed that people who have a strong preference for using this intelligence often choose careers or pleasure as engineers, auditors, chemists, and physicists.

To encourage the use of this intelligence with adults, do the following:
- Provide an outline.
- Begin with questions.
- Ask the participants what they think will happen and why.
- Use timelines.
- Provide, or invite the students to provide, as much background information as possible.
- Provide a list of questions or things to look for in the lesson.
- Ask the students to make connections between the Bible and life.
- Ask the students what they might do in the situation you are discussing.
- Ask the students to put the events of the story in order—what happened first, second, third, and so forth.
- Examine cause and effect.
- Ask the students to consider what might have happened if different choices had been made at any point.
- Use deductive reasoning (beginning with the whole and breaking it into understandable parts).
- Use inductive reasoning (using parts to discover the whole).

Spatial Learning (Visual-Spatial)

Spatial learners have the ability to picture something in their minds and then perform actions on that image (rotate it, add something to it, change its size, and so forth). Because spatial intelligence often is closely tied to visual observations, it is referred to as visual-spatial.

To a visual-spatial learner, a picture is worth a thousand words, because they think in patterns, colors, and shapes. When we can see something, our vision adds a depth of understanding not possible with words alone. Creative visual-spatial learners believe that if they can see it, they can make it happen. Creating often begins as a visual in our minds and is then created on paper, canvas, stone, wood, or another medium. As we seek to know where we are going as a church, an organization, a family, we often talk of creating a vision statement, a verbal picture of what we are about. Visual symbols are used worldwide for communication when language becomes a barrier.

People who learn best visually-spatially love to see pictures, maps, slides, and videos, because they can understand something more clearly if they can see it. This intelligence also incorporates the ability to image, to see in your mind's eye. Visual-spatial learners often draw pictures, graphs, or other diagrams as a way of note taking. I have observed that people who have a strong preference for using this intelligence often choose careers or pleasure as artists, designers of clothing, advertisers, book or magazine illustrators, photographers, video camera operators, and mapmakers.

To encourage the use of this intelligence with adults, do the following:
- Use pictures, slides, video clips, cartoons, symbols, and icons.
- Provide objects as a focal point of the lesson.
- Invite the students to change seats so that they can see from a different perspective.
- Use guided imagery (telling a story while students see it in their mind's eye).
- Provide a lighted candle to focus on during prayer.
- Use maps to identify places mentioned in your lesson or to trace a journey.
- Use timelines.
- Use a continuum (a line with Choice A on the left end and Choice B on the right end) and ask the participants to make a selection somewhere on the line.
- Use newsprint or a chalkboard.
- Have an outline and cross off what you have completed.
- Color-code handouts, outlines, and so forth.
- Use lighting to create atmosphere.
- Say things such as, "Close your eyes and imagine..."

Learning Through Music (Musical/Rhythmic)

Musical learners are sensitive to tone, melody, rhythm, pitch, and timbre. They think in lyrics and melody and are able to relate sounds to emotions and personality traits.

A colleague and I staged an encounter in front of our undergraduate students using no words, just numbers (one, two, three, and so forth). We went from a friendly greeting, to an uncomfortable disclosure, to a confrontation, to a friendly departure. It was the tone of our voices that presented the message to the class. They understood exactly what was happening and could relate to each stage of the encounter. We learn much from the tone and rhythm of speaking, sometimes more than from the words themselves.

Music can be used to enhance all areas of learning. People who learn best using this intelligence love to learn through music. Music speaks to them, sets a mood, aids in understanding. These learners often will tap out a rhythm literally or tap it in their heads. They like background music and learn best when music is incorporated. I have observed that people who have a strong preference for using this intelligence often choose careers or pleasure as musicians, vocalists, writers or teachers of music, and band or choir directors.

To encourage the use of this intelligence with adults, do the following:
- Sing.
- Select favorite hymns or songs and tell why they were chosen.

- Use music as background.
- Write new words to familiar hymns or songs.
- Pray the hymns.
- Set prayers to music.
- Set selected psalms to rhythms.
- Create a rap about your lesson.
- Open or close with a hymn or song that reflects the content of the lesson.
- Experience different styles of music and respond to the feelings that are evoked.
- Invite the students to discuss music that has helped them grow in faith.
- Teach a song that relates to the lesson.
- Use chants in the classroom.

Learning Through Physical Movement (Bodily-Kinesthetic)

We come to know our world through our body experiences. There is a connection between the mind and the body, our thoughts and our actions. Many athletes and dancers spend time visualizing their performances. By seeing in their mind's eye what they want their bodies to do, their performances are enhanced. We can learn to read body language.

People who learn best though physical movement need to move physically and to manipulate objects. These people like to play with a pencil or paper clip. They like to mold and shape and create with their hands. I have observed that people who have a strong preference for using this intelligence often choose careers or pleasure as athletes, dancers, mimes, physical education teachers, coaches, and construction workers.

To encourage the use of this intelligence with adults, do the following:
- Provide opportunities for physical movement.
- Give the students an object representing the theme of the lesson to handle as they pray or read.
- Use body prayer—raise your arms, turn your face upward, bow your head, touch your heart, kneel.
- Use roleplays.
- Perform a dramatic reading.
- Dance.

Learning Through Understanding Others (Interpersonal)

Interpersonal intelligence involves the capacity to understand the intentions, motivations, and desires of other people. People with strong interpersonal intelligence usually are able to work well with others.

In today's world, *cooperation* is a key word. In order to exist in a global society, we must learn to work and live together. We need to value and learn from diversity. With the explosion of information, no one person, organization, or church can know everything. To become more-effective learners, we must learn to practice the art of synergy (together we are better than any of us alone). Working and learning together is foundational to a successful family, career, church, or organization. When people work together effectively, their minds seem to become wired together; they begin to think in the same patterns. People who learn best in this intelligence experience the concept of synergy. They love to work in pairs or groups because learning happens through dialogue or working together. They can empathize and tune into other people's moods and feelings easily. I have observed that people who have a strong preference for using this intelligence often choose careers or pleasure as tour guides, talk show hosts, teachers, heads of organizational teams, labor representatives, training and development personnel, and therapists.

To encourage the use of this intelligence with adults, do the following:

- Work in pairs or small groups.
- Use cooperative learning such as the jigsaw technique, in which each person in a group learns a specific piece of the information being studied and becomes the expert on that particular aspect. Each person then teaches the rest of the group about his or her area of expertise.
- Help create mentors. A simple form of mentoring involves pairing a member of the group with a new person in the class or church and having the mentor guide the new person and help him or her feel at home.
- Practice listening skills.
- Intentionally affirm one another (until it becomes a habit).
- Write a story about the lesson individually and in teams; then refine and present it together.
- Do research in teams for the lesson.
- Study a scriptural passage together and discuss the insights.

Learning Through Self-Understanding (Intrapersonal)

Just as people with strong interpersonal intelligence are able to understand the feelings and motivations of others, people with strong intrapersonal intelligence have a keen awareness of their own fears, desires, and abilities. They are able to use that self-knowledge to make decisions about their lives.

A lot is going on in our minds at different levels of functioning, but we often are too busy to take time to relax and focus inwardly to sort and process the information we have gathered. People who learn best in this intelligence often work best alone. They need time to reflect and consider, so do not expect quick answers from them. Their silence does not mean they are not learning; it means they are taking time to process information and make it real for them. They often have profound ideas when they are allowed to think things through at their own pace. I have observed that people who have a strong preference for using this intelligence often choose careers or pleasure related to counseling.

To encourage the use of this intelligence with adults, do the following:
- Allow silent time so that the students can think, reflect, and process information.
- Encourage the students to keep journals or reflection logs.
- Give the lesson title (Scripture or theme) for next week so that the students have time to think about the topic.
- Provide one-on-one or small-group discussion time so that each person has a chance to tell his or her thoughts.
- Use guided meditation with built-in pauses for reflection.

Ideas for Using Multiple Intelligences in the Classroom

Not all adults like to sit around a table and have a discussion or listen to a lecture. Understanding your adult students and slowly incorporating the use of various intelligences will gently ease them into greater depths of learning. Do not try to use every intelligence in every lesson. Try doing the following:
- Use several translations or paraphrases of the same Scripture.
- Discover facts that will give a richness of meaning to your lesson.
- Use maps or pictures to illuminate your lesson.
- Use a song that goes with the lesson.
- Bring an object that is related to the topic for each student to hold as he or she reflects.
- Provide opportunities for the students to talk with a partner or small group about what they are thinking or feeling.
- Ask the students to reflect on what the message says to them personally.
- Bring in objects from nature to help focus the lesson.

If you experiment with using other intelligences, you will be amazed at how the students respond. Begin with small changes, and ask the students to risk with you. Often, they will be amazed at their depth of expression and understanding when their favorite intelligences are tapped. Cast your bread upon the waters—it will come back buttered!

Some Things to Think About

1. Which intelligences do you normally include in a lesson?

2. Think about the members of your class or small group. List the names of your students, and then note which intelligences each person prefers using.

3. List at least three ways you can include additional intelligences in your next lessons.

Factors That Contribute to Learning

Now that you know something about how adults learn, let us turn to other factors that contribute to learning. This is a different focus, but it is not less important if we are to reach adult learners effectively, so that they may grow as disciples. There are many things to consider as you lead adults. Whether these considerations come naturally or are more-consciously intentional, all these factors affect what happens in your classroom.

Stages of Faith

Growth in faith is not something that is ever complete. Each person's faith journey is unique, yet there are some general things we know about how people come to and grow in faith. In his book *Will Our Children Have Faith?* (The Seabury Press, 1976), John Westerhoff proposes a theory that I believe is helpful in understanding how faith develops for many people.

Our faith begins as we soak up the sights, sounds, and images of faith. We attend worship and listen to the message and the music. We experience faith by living in an environment of sharing and interacting with people of faith. Westerhoff describes this as "experienced faith."

The next stage, "affiliative faith," is when we begin to identify with a particular church denomination or belief. Faith becomes our story and our way of life. We can say, "I belong to Rush United Methodist Church." At this stage, having a clear sense of identity and belonging to a group is important.

The next stage, "searching faith," is when we begin to ask questions that push, probe, and test our thoughts and ideas. We begin to wrestle with our faith and, like Jacob, might spend much time wrestling with God (Genesis 32:22-31).

The final stage, "owned faith," is when we can say confidently, "This is what I believe." We have lived enough summers to have experienced God's work in our lives and have come to a place of peace and understanding of who and whose we are. We live out a personal witness to our faith through actions and reach a place of spiritual health and identity.

All of your adult students will not be at the same place in their faith. Assure them that faith is faith and that there is no right or wrong faith and no precise way to work through the stages. Do not put a student on the spot about faith. You might explain these stages and create a visual on newsprint or on a chalkboard. Ask them to discuss in small groups when they have experienced any of the stages of faith. If students want to tell their faith stories, encourage (but do not force) them to do so.

Emotional Climate

Creating a safe emotional climate is critical for faith and in-depth learning to be experienced. Deep learning occurs when the emotions are engaged. A safe emotional environment grants the freedom to explore without fear of ridicule and allows faith to grow. An environment that is accepting, challenging, compassionate, caring, and spirit-filled leads to greater learning and faith sharing. It is helpful to establish a set of rules for a safe environment. Examples might include these:

- Confidentiality is respected.
- It is all right to pass.
- Say only what is comfortable.
- Respect one another's opinions.
- Agree to disagree.
- Say "ouch" when you feel your feelings have been stepped on.

Establishing ground rules helps to build trust and mutual respect. Use the rules suggested, or create your own as a group. Display your rules and live by them. When rules are broken, remind the students of the rules. Initiating rules will reap benefits as your class learns and grows together. If someone is unkind, you may stop the class and ask the person to whom the remark was intended, "Was that an ouch?" Sometimes the person making the remark is not aware of the hurt he or she may have caused. This attempt to make people think about their behavior helps everyone to become more aware of one another's feelings.

People will open up and tell about their lives only in an environment in which they feel safe and cared for. As the trust level builds, people will begin to tell about their deepest thoughts, fears, doubts, and beliefs. This is where faith grows. This is where lives are transformed. When we begin to tell our stories and listen to the stories of others, we deepen our understanding of who and whose we are. This deep kind of sharing takes time to develop; it does not happen overnight. Do not expect it to happen until you have developed a sense of trust and caring.

When people reach a deep level of trust and begin to speak from their hearts, emotions may surface that may be uncomfortable. If someone leaves the room, ask someone else to lead the discussion while you go after the person. Gently ask if he or she is all right and if there is anything you can do to help. Sometimes the person may need to be alone for a while. That is fine. Sometimes he or she may need to talk or cry in a more private setting. That is fine. However, you should personally make sure he or she is all right. Return to the classroom and tell the other students that the person is fine. The anxiety level of the class will remain high until there is some word of reassurance. Remind them of the confidentiality rule.

If someone cries in class, the way you respond will depend on the situation. If the person is crying tears of joy, help him or her celebrate. If the person is crying tears of sorrow, ask how the class can help. Sometimes, gently placing an arm around the person's shoulder or holding his or her hand is all that is needed. If the person is crying tears of hurt, ask the person to step outside the room; then help the person to calm down. Once the person is calm, decide on a path that will resolve the situation.

If a disagreement occurs in class, you may refer to your rules and remind them that the class agreed to respect one another's opinions. This does not mean everyone must agree; it means that everyone cares enough about one another to allow for differences. If a conflict situation can be dealt with at the very outset, it is easier to handle. This is why saying "ouch" is an important habit to establish. Often, we let the little ouches pass and then explode because someone has been pushing too hard. Encourage your students to express feelings of hurt or disagreement early on, when they can be handled easily. If a disagreement has gone beyond the early stage, you may ask one or both parties to leave the room, so that you can talk quietly with them. (Your tone of voice will set the direction.) In extreme instances, you may ask for help from other members of the class.

If the disagreement is in the form of theological differences, you might review your ground rules and agree to disagree or to respect one another's opinions. If either of these methods does not work, call the group together and find areas of common ground. Find things on which you can agree; then work from there. You might remind them that we all are on a journey of understanding of how we best can live out our Christian lives.

Most teachers or leaders of adults are not trained counselors; therefore, your role is not to provide professional counseling. If needed, you may offer to help the person find professional help or offer to provide a listening ear.

Group Building

Adults need a minute or two to disengage themselves from the rest of the week and their hectic schedules and to center and focus on where they are. Beginning each session with a warm-up or icebreaker is a way to help this process. Always begin with questions that are nonthreatening and that help people find a level playing field. As time goes on, your questions can delve deeper into faith issues and beliefs. (See "Learning Hooks, on pages 12–15.) Never put students on the spot in group building by asking questions that will embarrass them if they do not know the answer. This process of beginning with a warm-up will yield untold rewards in terms of growing faith. Some examples of group-building questions include:

- What is your earliest memory of the church?
- Who has helped you on your faith journey?
- What was the best advice you ever received?

All of these questions can be answered by anyone. Students do not have to have biblical knowledge or any expertise to answer them. The questions level the playing field.

As your group gets more comfortable and the trust level builds, you might ask questions such as these:
- What was your most embarrassing moment?
- What is your greatest fear?
- Who is your greatest role model?
- What is your wish for the world?

You may eventually ask learning-hook questions related to your class study as a warm-up. Questions may include these:
- How are you like Peter (or whomever you are studying)?
- What biblical character do you relate to, and why?
- If you could ask Jesus one question, what would it be?
- When have you felt God's presence?
- Where in nature do you see God?
- When was the last time you thanked God for something ordinary?
- When have you experienced a miracle?

Remember that group-building questions help build the group into a trusting, loving, learning community. Be careful and gentle in your questions. The questions are a way to help adult students focus on being in a faith-forming setting and leaving other business behind for an hour or so.

Look for ways to connect your opening questions with the lesson for the day. Once the group is mature enough in levels of trust and comfort, intentional group building is a wonderful way to encourage them to share their faith journey.

Set a time limit for this process. You may ask for a total-group response to your question by saying, "You will each have thirty seconds to tell us about…" If you have a large class or people who are more comfortable speaking in small groups, you may choose to break them into small groups or partners. Say something such as, "Talk to the person next to you for one minute about…" or "Find a person you have not talked with for a while and for the next sixty seconds discuss…"

Teachable Moments

Sometimes you will need to put aside your plan for the day. If the group needs to deal with an issue—a death, a tragedy, a joyful time in the faith community—then sacrifice your plan, wonderful as it may be, and go with the issue of immediate concern. God will understand and approve! In teachable moments, processing the issue (asking for feelings, insights, common experiences) is essential for deep learning to occur.

Some Things to Think About

1. What stage of faith seems to describe where you are currently? In what stage are the members of your class?

2. List four things you can do to help the members of your class feel emotionally safe.

3. How might you respond if a class member ridicules another class member's idea?

4. What are some ways you might respond if someone cries or becomes emotionally upset during class?

5. List five group-building questions you have used or plan to use.

Physical Climate

Adults respond to the room's physical climate, which includes many areas. Your meeting room speaks volumes. A room with Christmas decorations up in March says, "No one cares." An attractive space says, "Someone does care." Your classroom sets a mood and creates an atmosphere for learning. You can control some things; other things you cannot control. Work with what you have to make it the best environment you can provide.

Walls and Furnishings

If you are leading a lively discussion group, comfortable chairs arranged in a circle are conducive to learning. If you are leading a study where people need to read and write, tables and chairs work best. Make sure adults have seating that is the appropriate size.

Too much clutter on the walls or on furnishings is distracting. However, a focal point such as a picture, cross, candle, or other symbol may help establish a mood for learning. Maps or illustrations can help to reinforce learning. Plants can provide a sense of beauty and serenity. Small objects (paper clips, pencils, telephone wires, simple toys) are helpful for those who like to fiddle with something in their hands.

Heat, Light, and Sound

If the room is too hot or too cold, adults will be more concerned about their physical comfort than about learning. The students will have difficulty concentrating if the sun is directly in their eyes or if the light is too dim for them to see their reading material.

Sound can be a positive or negative factor. Close off as much distracting noise as possible. Music can add to the learning climate if it is used wisely. Create a mood (from upbeat to meditative) by playing appropriate music.

Accessibility

Can anyone who wishes physically get into your classroom? Can you accommodate someone in a wheelchair or on crutches? Can everyone hear and see well? Not all church buildings are totally accessible, so you may need to create a space that will allow everyone to be welcome. Large-print materials are available or can be made available. Seating people with special needs in places to best meet their needs is a prime consideration.

Beverages

Some people cannot learn without a cup of coffee. Having beverages such as coffee, tea, and water available says you care about your students.

Some Things to Think About

1. What messages would your classroom give a newcomer?

2. How is your classroom comfortable for your students?

3. Name the aspects of your classroom that make it conducive to learning.

4. Name the aspects of your classroom that hinder learning.

5. What changes can you make to your classroom that will enhance learning?

6. How does the physical climate of your classroom show you care about your students?

Social and Intellectual Needs

Some adults enjoy learning in a conversational and relaxed mood, where there is much laughter and telling of life stories in a light-hearted way. These students are open to poetry, guided imagery, and music to enhance their learning. Social time is a critical part of their learning. Time around the coffeepot is not wasted.

Other adults want and need a more-structured and academic environment, where there is a more-serious tone to learning. These people thrive on cognitive, rational learning and often think that anything other than serious Bible study is frivolous and a waste of time. Adults may shop around until they find a group that meets their intellectual as well as social needs. This does not mean that learning does not take place in both settings; it just happens in a different way. Both kinds of learners need to have some balance of cognition and flexibility.

It makes sense to pair teachers and students according to their preferred styles. Placing a structured teacher with students who learn best in a relaxed, free-flowing atmosphere will frustrate everyone. Students learn best when the teaching style matches their learning style.

Some adult classes are not really classes at all. One group met in a small library-type room on Sundays to talk about the morning's headlines and how they affected their lives. Their curriculum was the Sunday paper, which they enjoyed discussing with one another. The group was informal and had no designated teacher, but they were a group. They cared about one another; and as trust levels grew, they brought issues of faith into their discussion of the headlines.

Some adult classes meet beyond the walls of the church. Restaurants or homes make interesting alternatives for some adult classes. Not everyone must meet in the church. A corner table in a nearby fast food restaurant might do well as a space for adults to learn.

In one community, a group of Christians from various churches meet once a week in the cafeteria of a large company for lunch and Bible study. In another community, a group of men meet for Bible study on Wednesdays at six-thirty in the morning. There is no right time or place to have an adult class gather for faith growth. One of the most critical learnings for churches is that Sunday morning is not the only time you can learn about God.

Classes do not have to be large. Jesus said, "For where two or three are gathered in my name, I am there among them" (Matthew 18:20). I believe Jesus was less concerned about numbers than about sharing faith. Some small groups provide a safe place to talk and listen. Sometimes great learning and faith sharing happens over a cup of coffee in someone's kitchen.

Some Things to Think About

1. How does your church choose what small groups and classes will be offered?

2. How would you describe your preferred teaching style?

3. List the formal and informal classes and groups provided by your church. Where and when do these classes and groups occur?

4. List three new possibilities of classes or groups you would like your church to explore.

5. Use the "Learning Needs Inventory" on the following page to help you evaluate your own attitudes about adult learning.

Learning Needs Inventory

Please rank the responses to each question from 1 (first choice) to 4 (last choice).

Adult learning is
___ serious
___ an opportunity for growth
___ a way to connect with others
___ a way to learn about the Bible and how it connects to my life

I learn best when
___ the atmosphere is relaxed
___ the course has an outline to be followed
___ I know where we are going with the learning
___ I can apply the learning to my daily life

The most important thing an adult class does is
___ study the Bible
___ grow in community
___ learn new things
___ provide a path for my faith journey

The teacher should
___ have the answers to questions raised by class members
___ be flexible and meet the needs of the students
___ be prepared
___ learn with the class members

Bible study is
___ important to my understanding of who I am as a child of God
___ a way for me to tell about my faith
___ a serious matter
___ a way to interpret God's meaning for my life

Fellowship is
___ a way to connect with people
___ time around the coffeepot
___ the five minutes before class
___ a necessary part of faith growth

I would like to participate in an adult class on
___ in-depth Bible study
___ contemporary issues
___ applying the Bible to my daily life
___ social concerns

Teaching and Learning

Teaching and learning are not the same things. Often, what you think is being taught is not necessarily what is being learned. Adult students come with their own agendas and will connect learning to what is going on in their lives. Ten people may hear ten different meanings in a single lesson.

Students may listen and even discuss what they have learned, but their understanding and application of hearing God's Word comes as they live out the lesson in actual or simulated experience. Passive learning is not what we are about. We aim to create Christian disciples who learn and live God's Word.

Often, God calls us to teach what we most need to learn. I hear over and over again that teachers learned so much as they prepared to teach. Doing the background work, checking resources, anticipating questions, and finding answers is an incredible learning experience. God blesses us as we teach God's people.

Some Ways to Evaluate What Is Being Learned

- Encourage students to keep a journal of learning, and periodically ask for volunteers to tell what they wrote.
- At the close of class ask for people to list new insights they have gained.
- Have group members create a wire sculpture that illustrates what they have learned.
- Ask the students to name a color or a fruit that describes their learning.
- Ask the students to say a word or phrase that expresses how God touched them through the class.
- Put up a poster-size piece of paper and ask the students to make notes on it (graffiti style) about what they have learned.

Responsibility for Learning

Adults learn what they choose to learn because they are responsible for their own learning. In church settings there are no formal tests to show what students have learned and no grade levels to be completed or degrees to be worked toward. Adult students do not have to be there. They choose to come to a class because they have an interest in what is being taught and believe it will enrich their lives in some way. (Colleges and universities call these students nontraditional students, and professors love them.)

This desire to learn is based on intrinsic motivation, which means that people make choices based on inner desires. They do something because they want to, for no outward reward. Extrinsic motivation means that choices are made based on an outward reward, such as a grade, a degree, a promotion.

The Teacher's Role

A favorite professor of mine had a T-shirt that said "Those who can teach; those who cannot find some less-significant form of work." A play on an old cliché, to be sure—profound truth as well.

Contrast that statement with "No one ever teaches anything of any significance." Equally true. Is it a paradox? Not really. If a teacher really understands his or her role, the statements support each other. A teacher's role is to facilitate learning in the student. It is the teacher's job to provide opportunity for each student to make discoveries and connect the new learning in meaningful ways to his or her personal life.

A teacher's role is not to be the keeper of the answers; therefore, the teacher does not need to be the expert. God often calls us to teach what we most need to learn. You are a co-learner. Granted, you must be prepared and have the skills for guiding the group through the process, but your role is to be open to the Holy Spirit and to be willing to be a learner as well.

The teacher facilitates the creation of a sense of community in the class or group. Creating community through caring, sharing, listening, and celebrating should be a priority of every session. The growing of community is a sign that Christian education has taken place. It is up to the teacher to provide a safe environment, a challenging course of study, and a method of presentation that fosters self-discovery.

The teacher is a catalyst who prepares the way for students to find God within themselves. Teachers must let go of the need for immediate and visible results from their teaching. They must be flexible and willing to let God's presence shine through the lesson.

Curriculum Resources

Curriculum resources can be a teacher's best friend or worst enemy. Resources provide a guide, but you usually will need to adapt curriculum to meet the specific needs of your class. Literally hundreds of pieces of adult curricula are available, ranging from pieces that focus on the transmission of information to pieces that are experiential and process-oriented.

As you select curriculum resources, consider the needs and makeup of the class. Ask yourself questions: *Do the students have a deep desire to know facts about the Bible? Are they used to structure? Do they like to get information from the teacher? Do they prefer lecture or small-group discussion? What are the life issues they are dealing with?* Then select a curriculum resource that reflects their needs.

Consider the teacher's needs and style. Trying to force a laid-back teacher into a structured curriculum will frustrate both teacher and students. Teachers need to spend some time reviewing curriculum and making choices.

Questions to ask as you evaluate curriculum resources include these:

- Does the curriculum include methods that consider the different ways that people learn?
- Is the curriculum user-friendly? (Can you pick it up and work with it easily? Does it provide background information for the teacher? Does it offer options and choices of ways to present the information?)
- What is the underlying theology of the curriculum, and is it consistent with the theology of your class? (What assumptions does the piece make about the nature of God? How does the piece interpret the authority and role of Scripture, tradition, experience, and reason? What assumptions does the piece make about our relationship with God?)
- Does the curriculum include time for prayer and worship?

I have always told teachers that I did not care if they took one week or six weeks to complete a lesson. A good combination of teacher/learner/Holy Spirit will allow curriculum to form itself around the learners' needs. It is far more important for adult learners to make discoveries and become transformed than to complete a piece of curriculum in a given amount of time. It is more important to provide an opportunity for them to experience God's presence in their lives than to learn facts. Briefly stated, less is more.

Knowing Your Class

Good teachers can read the mood of the class and make adjustments, which sometimes means putting aside a planned lesson. Dealing with an event in the life of the congregation or in the life of an individual is more important than the lesson you have prepared. These events may be joyful occasions that lend themselves to celebration or sad situations that require love and support.

Learn to watch for nonverbal messages from members of your class and react accordingly. Much of our communication is nonverbal, so train yourself to be observant. Watch for signals of lack of eye contact, closed-in body posture (arms folded tightly, head down, slumped position), foot or finger tapping. If you see someone acting in a way that is different from his or her normal behavior, quietly ask if he or she is all right. If the person chooses to talk about what is on his or her mind, listen with minimum input. If he or she chooses not to talk, ask if you can hold him or her in prayer and if you can ask the class for prayers. Always ask permission to bring a private issue to the class, even if it is just asking for prayer.

A built-in time for joys and concerns or prayer requests may bring these issues to the group in a natural way. The trust level of the group will determine how deeply people will go in asking for prayers. As a teacher, you can model praying for others.

Some Things to Think About

1. List three methods you use, or plan to use, to help determine what is being learned.

2. List five qualities you believe a good teacher should possess.

3. How are curriculum resources selected for your class?

4. What are the strengths of the curriculum resources you are using? What are the weaknesses?

5. What clues do you look for to help you read your class?

6. What would help you to know your students better?

Faith Formation

Means of Grace

Teachers and leaders cannot effectively help others grow in their faith unless they are growing. One significant way of being continually formed in faith is to practice the means of grace, which are channels by which we experience God's love. Although God touches our lives in many ways, a number of particular practices have been helpful to Christians throughout history. The early Methodists described these practices in the General Rules of the Methodist societies. Briefly stated, the means of grace include avoiding evil, doing good, worship, Bible study, Holy Communion, prayer, fasting, and Christian conversation.

Small Groups

Small groups have been a part of Methodism since its beginnings. John Wesley, the founder of the Methodist movement, initiated class meetings that met weekly to witness and watch over one another in Christian love. They talked about their faith, held one another accountable, and prayed for one another.

In recent years, there has been renewed interest in the role small groups play in forming faith. Having been a part of a small group that has met weekly for nearly two years, I can testify to the power of small groups. Small groups are the backbone of formational faith. When we get together with the same people regularly, we share our lives, our faith, our laughter and tears, our prayer needs, and our accountability to one another and to God. We wrestle with Scripture and how it touches our lives today. We agree to disagree and learn from one another's beliefs. We witness to God's working in our lives, and we grow in faith.

We know that this intimate gathering and sharing is biologically and spiritually necessary. As humans, we need that kind of intimate contact with others because our bodies and spirits would wither without it.

Small groups may form around areas of hobbies or interests, gender issues, life-span issues (young adults or parents of young children), service to the church or community, and so forth. From a faith-forming perspective, the stated focus of the group is not as important as meeting on a regular basis, sharing lives, sharing faith (many faith stories are told in an informal way at our quilting group), and praying.

Small groups will have a life span. Some may be years, some a matter of months. It depends on the group, the group's focus, and the commitment of those involved. I believe that when a group has formed, bonded, and grown together to build a trust level where real sharing happens, the addition of a new person totally changes the group. There is no longer a shared history. The group must begin to reform, and there always will be a difference between those who were original members and the newcomers. In many situations, it is more effective to help new people begin a small group of their own rather than to try to incorporate them into an existing group.

Formational Teaching

When we teach formationally, we are inviting people to make life-changing decisions. We are not simply transferring information. We are helping adults to take the Scripture and live it, to walk their talk, to act on their faith. We are transforming lives. Many adults are searching for answers to the burning question "Is that all there is?" Some are challenging materialistic, shallow, opulent lifestyles and finding them wanting. To reach adults in transformational ways, we must help them to apply scriptural messages. Simply knowing the story is not enough. We must continually ask these questions:

- How will my life be changed by this knowledge?
- How is God acting in this situation?
- Where have I experienced God's grace this week?
- How am I living out my faith?
- What can I do to be a better follower of Christ?

We must learn the difference between knowing who Jesus is and inviting him into our lives. We must not only learn about the Bible but also live the Bible. We are about making disciples.

Prayer

Adult classes need to include a time of prayer, for it is foundational to our connection with God. We can practice different forms of prayer and encourage students to pray during the week. Help your students learn to pray in various ways. Encourage them to pray often, and remind them that there is no right or wrong way to pray. Experiment with some of these prayer ideas:

- Begin and end each session with prayer.
- Invite students to lead prayers. (Ask for volunteers, but never force anyone to pray out loud.)
- Initiate a time of silent prayer, which is safe for everyone.
- Develop prayer partners. (Pair up people who agree to pray for each other every day. They may change partners each month or continue with the same ones indefinitely. They also may write their names on slips of paper and draw out the name of someone in your class to pray for. Again, they may change names periodically.)

- Discover the benefits of breath prayer. (Think of what you call God and what you most want from God. Put those things together in a prayer that is from five to seven words long and can be done in conjunction with your breathing. The first few words are thought as you breath in; the rest are thought as you breath out. For example, "Grant me your peace, O God." The benefits of this type of prayer are manifold: You can pray this prayer anywhere, anytime. It has a calming effect when you are under stress. It is a reassurance that God is close all the time.)
- Introduce the ACTS model of prayer to your class. (This model includes four components: *A* stands for *adoration and praise,* *C* for *confession,* *T* for *thanksgiving,* and *S* for *supplication.*)
- Create a place for students to record prayer requests. (Providing a box with paper and pencils gives the students an easy way to make a written request for prayers while remaining anonymous.)
- Invite students to keep a private prayer journal, in which they record prayer requests, stories about prayers, favorite prayers, and so forth.

Some Things to Think About

1. Which means of grace do you practice on a regular basis?

2. Which means of grace would you like to explore in greater depth?

3. How is faith formation occurring in the small groups in your congregation? How could faith formation in these groups be enhanced?

4. How can you encourage transformational learning?

5. List three ways to challenge or hold your students accountable for living their faith.

6. List five ways you incorporate, or plan to incorporate, prayer into your class.

Teaching Methods

As stated earlier in this book, people learn in many ways. Using different methods in your teaching will create a learning environment that appeals to the different ways people learn. The following sections briefly describe three methods that can be used effectively in a variety of settings.

Storytelling

So much of faith growth involves telling our stories and listening to the faith stories of others. By sharing our encounters with the living God, we reaffirm our own faith and help others to grow in faith. This kind of storytelling happens when we feel safe and loved. We then will risk talking about our fears, doubts, joys, and celebrations. When we trust one another, we are willing to talk about our relationship with God, which strengthens us as well as our listeners. When we listen to others' stories, we support and verify their relationship with God.

Storytelling is a powerful way for adults to learn. Some methods that encourage people to tell their stories include these:

- Use open-ended questions.
- Ask students to choose a favorite hymn or Scripture verse and to tell why it is important to them.
- Invite students to tell a personal story of how they came to faith.
- Invite students to tell about a time when they felt close to or far from God.
- Create a timeline marked with decades. (Ask the students to write on the timeline significant times in their lives and how they were changed by these events. Ask how the events changed the way they look at God and at their faith.)

Do not expect adult students to do in-depth storytelling until they feel safe and loved. Again, begin with nonthreatening questions or topics. As the class becomes a community, storytelling may be a natural part of the class. Every time a student tells a faith story, he or she relives it and reinforces his or her faith. Remember the ground rule that says it is all right to pass. Never ask anyone to talk until he or she is ready and willing to do so.

Lecture

Some adults learn best through lectures. Lecture does not mean reading from notes without making eye contact or having students involved. For a lecture to be most successful, consider the following guidelines:

- Have a clear focus, with one or two main areas of content. When the lecture wanders all over the place, the listeners get frustrated.
- Have a concise statement of purpose and know what you hope to accomplish by the end of the session.

- Move from "What?" (the information), to "So What?" (how the information connects to life today), to "Now What?" (how my life will be changed by this information).
- Structure time for interaction. (Ask questions, pause at times during the lecture, and ask the students to talk to the person next to them for a few minutes about the information.)
- Include personal experiences and stories to make the lecture come alive.
- Welcome questions and take time (without getting totally off track) to answer, acknowledge, and respect students' queries.
- Begin and end on time. (This does not mean that discussion cannot continue beyond the class time. If people are really engaged, they may want to continue their thinking and discussion. However, you must honor the time of students who must be elsewhere.)
- Make eye contact as you lecture.
- Vary your tone of voice so that you will not speak in a monotone voice.
- End with a "Now What?" climax that challenges hearers to reflect on how this information will be used in their lives.

Asking Questions

Many adults think best when they are discussing questions. There are helpful ways of asking questions that will stimulate learning and keep people at ease. A good question nudges thinking, opens us to new ways of thinking, and leads to new questions. We miss out on great learning opportunities when we fail to ask questions or when we provide answers too readily. Discussing questions is a powerful way to get to know ourselves and others better. Consider a good question to be a door to conversation. Jesus asked questions as a way to encourage people to think for themselves, and he often answered a question with a question. Consider these guidelines:

- Avoid questions with a simple yes, no, or one-word answer. (These questions shut down rather than stimulate thinking. Ask open or probing questions that require some analyzing and critical thinking.)
- Allow for reflection time. (Ask a question and then plan for a full minute of time to think. Some adults need this time to process the question. Some adults jump right in with an answer, and those who need time never have an opportunity to tell their thoughts.)
- Look for lots of right answers. (Ask questions that engage people, and invite them to consider several alternatives. You will set a model for this kind of thinking if you respond by saying, "Let's make a list of as many right answers as we can." Or set a goal by saying, "Let's see if we can come up with three right answers to this question." If you ask questions that have one right answer, it shuts down thinking and pondering.)

- Ask "What If?" and "Why?" questions to make students think of alternative answers. (Sometimes these questions will lead to wonderful and faith-filled answers. For example, "What if Mary had said no to the angel?" or "Why, do you think, did the angel come to lowly shepherds instead of to priests at the Temple?")
- Employ think time. (Tell your students that thinking takes time. Explain that often you will ask a probing question and allow a full minute—time it—for people to think and reflect on their answers. Occasionally, you might ask them to write answers before stating them. These techniques allow time for everyone to gather their thoughts and may prevent only a few people from always having the answers.)
- Avoid evaluating students' answers. (As soon as you, the teacher, respond with "Right" or "Good answer," everyone else will have no need to think any further. You might consider saying, "Thank you" or "That's one right answer. Does anyone else have another?" or giving a simple nod. These responses from you acknowledge that the students have been heard, without passing judgment and shutting down the thinking of others.)
- Encourage students' questions. (You may explain at the beginning that you will take questions at any time, or you may stop periodically to ask if anyone has questions.)
- Respect students' questions. (There is no such thing as a dumb question. If you act like the students' questions are dumb, the students will immediately stop asking questions. Saying things such as, "That's a good question" or "I never thought of it that way" shows students you respect and honor their questions.)
- Reserve your opinions for the end of the discussion. (You might say something such as, "Let's see what the rest of the class thinks first." By doing this, you participate but do not dominate or close down thinking. After all students have had a chance to tell their thoughts, you may add your information and insights as part of the group process. You do not need to be the keeper of the answers. It is perfectly fine, and sometimes appropriate, to say, "I don't know. Let's find out together" or "I'm not sure. Can anyone do the research?")
- Use different types of questions for different purposes. (When accurate information is required, use information questions, such as "How many disciples did Jesus have?" Comprehension questions, such as "Why, do you think, did Jesus choose those particular men?" help students consider the significance of the information. Application questions, such as "If Jesus called you to be a disciple, what do you think your response would have been?" help students apply the learning to their own lives. Analysis questions, such as "Which of the disciples do you identify with

most?" encourage students to think deeply about the issues involved. Synthesis questions, such as "How might the story be different if Judas had not betrayed Jesus?" help students to consider new possibilities. Evaluation questions, such as "Have you ever denied Jesus by action or inaction?" help students evaluate their own lives in light of what they have learned.

Some Things to Think About

1. How do you encourage students to tell their faith stories?

2. How might you encourage students to take their stories beyond the walls of your classroom?

3. List four ways you involve, or plan to involve, your students when you lecture.

4. List three ways you incorporate asking questions into your teaching.

5. Write out a series of thought-provoking questions to keep handy during your lesson.

6. Find at least six of the questions Jesus asked. Analyze them and consider what they did for the learners.

Diversity in the Classroom

One of the key areas of our culture today in business, entertainment, and the church is the realization and acknowledgment of diversity. We are a diverse society. Even within a seemingly homogeneous church community, there is a multitude of diversity. Being aware of and sensitive to diversity helps us to be better teachers.

Cultural Diversity

With the exception of Native Americans, we all have come from somewhere else. It may have been many generations ago, but we bring customs, beliefs, values, and morals with us through our heritage. It might be interesting to discover how your class is diverse. Ask about customs around celebrating church holidays, and invite the students to bring in dishes or mementos that speak of their heritage. Enjoy learning from one another.

Economic Diversity

Being sensitive to economic status means not making assumptions that all your students can contribute to a mission project or purchase study books or take field trips. Students can become embarrassed when economic decisions are made without consulting the class. Have a plan to provide scholarship help if it is needed. (Do this quietly and without causing embarrassment.) Sometimes the people who have the least give the most.

Learning Diversity

Pay attention to the way your students learn best. Review "Multiple Intelligences" (pages 19–25). Be aware of the way your students respond to teaching styles and methods. Be sure to vary your lessons to accommodate all learning needs.

Faith Diversity

Remember that not everyone is at the same place in his or her faith journey. When questions of belief arise, open the questions to the group in an exploratory and nonjudgmental way. Remind them of the agreements they have regarding how they will treat one another. Invite them to listen for the Holy Spirit.

Personal Diversity

Just as no two fingerprints are the same, no two personalities are the same. It is critical to know who your students are and to realize that they are different. They will not all be pleased with the same things. You cannot help that. Awareness is key. There are so many issues that affect the comfort and safety level of adult learners. Some adults are open and eager to learn; others are ill at ease and afraid of looking foolish. You, as leader, set the tone of the class, provide a safe environment for learning, model respect for all opinions, and help adults grow in faith. You have an awesome task. God has called you to teach God's people and will provide the gifts you need. Trust and claim the call and the gifts. Ask for God's help in teaching, and then just do it! Accept the fact that your students are diverse. Love them for it. Learn from it. Grow with the richness that diversity provides. Thank God for the infinite wisdom of diversity.

Some Things to Think About

1. List at least four ways your students are diverse.

2. Record ways you can use the diverse nature of your students to enrich the class.

3. List three ways to affirm diversity in your class.

Section Two
So What?

You Teach Real People

The material in the previous section provided a lot of information. As you read it, you probably learned some new things and were reminded of things you have known for a long time. Knowing the ways people learn, effective teaching techniques, ways to plan a lesson, and so forth are all important. But it is just as important to know the people in your class and to understand the life and faith issues with which they are dealing.

In this section, you will meet some real people. Their names and minor details have been changed, but their stories are true. They are not unique. You have a Ben or a Joyce in your church, too. No two circumstances are exactly alike, but you have people who are single parents, people who are suffering from some form of loss, people who are quiet and reflective, people who need the church to help them in times of crisis. I invite you to read each person's story and then substitute the names and situations of people in your class. Using the questions provided, reflect on how you might be in ministry to and with the specific people in your class or small group.

Perhaps the questions will trigger other questions for you. The goal of using profiles is to help you get a clearer picture of who is in your class, what their needs are, and how you (and your church) might help them to grow in faith. As you read the stories, consider what you are doing, or might do, to meet the needs of adults in your church who fit into similar categories.

The people in the profiles are at different ages and stages of life and faith. They represent some of the major types of adults in your church. Each type has unique needs. It is important for you, as a leader of adults, to begin to realize where these needs can be grouped for the best faith growth to happen. It also is important to realize that special needs sometimes require special care.

Ben

Ben is a thirty-five-year-old single father of a five-year-old son. His wife died of breast cancer a year ago, and he is trying to be a good father and find a life for himself. He is struggling with a big question: Why did God let his wife, who was a faith-filled and God-centered person, die a horrible and painful death? Where was God's mercy?

Ben is part of an adult Sunday school class and is trying to remain faithful for himself and his son. He is still staggering under the loss of his wife and best friend.

As you consider ways you might be in ministry with people like Ben, consider the following suggestions:

- Intentionally work to create a community and sense of trust in your class.
- Encourage those who have suffered loss to join a support group.
- Encourage the students to tell about their feelings at the beginning of each class time.
- Provide a bibliography of books on loss, or have the books available in your church library.
- Keep a list of groups in your community that provide counseling and other support for those experiencing loss.

Ben is a single parent. Parents, both single and couples, need a place to discuss what is wonderful and frustrating about being a parent. They need to know they are not alone. Single parents in particular need to be with people with whom they can talk and learn.

Some things to consider might include these:

- As the class is gathering, be intentional about inquiring how their children are doing.
- If the class plans social gatherings, consider ways the entire family can be involved.
- Include opportunities during class prayer time to offer joys and concerns for family members.

Ben is a quiet, thoughtful, private man. During class discussions, people often offer answers and opinions immediately without waiting to give the quiet, thoughtful types like Ben time to speak. Remaining silent does not mean that these people are not thinking or reflecting. Sometimes they will come up with a wonderful insight or thought-provoking question if they are given time to reflect and respond. Often, they do not have that chance because the class has moved on six paces.

Some strategies that are particularly helpful for people who need reflection time include these:

- Pause for a moment of silent reflection two or three times during your class period.
- Provide a thought-provoking question for next week to allow the students a week to think.
- Break into small groups and take a silent break before you begin the discussion.
- Write out questions and have them available as people come into the classroom.

Some Things to Think About

1. Picture each person in your class, and think about what you know about their losses. Have any of them lost a loved one, a job (accompanied by loss of self-esteem and sense of worth), a sense of something to live for?

2. Write the names of those in your class who have suffered some form of loss. What do you do to help people deal with loss and still remain faith-filled? What have you tried already? How can you make these discoveries without prying into personal space?

3. How does your church provide opportunities for single parents to attend church functions and feel welcome and part of the church family? How can you provide time for parents to tell their stories, their tips on child rearing, their baby sitters' names, their willingness to help one another?

4. How do you provide for the people in your classes who are quiet and need time to reflect?

Dan and Carol

Dan and Carol are in their early forties, are college educated, have professional careers, and are parents of three children. They moved to their community seven years ago and immediately began looking for a church. They expected several needs to be met by the faith community in which they raised their children. Dan and Carol had grown up in different denominations and had no particular denominational loyalty. They had been raised in the church as children and had memories of youth groups and lasting friendships. They both had stopped going to church during college and had returned when they had children, so that they would have a Christian education. Their two oldest children are teenagers and present the normal challenges of that age group. Dan and Carol are trying to be good faith role models, parents, and providers.

When Carol first came to the church, her youngest child (now ten years old) was in the church nursery. Carol inspected the nursery and found it to be the most suitable, though not perfect, of all the nurseries in the churches they had visited. The issue of a clean, safe nursery was a large part of their choice of a church.

Carol and Dan love upbeat music and a lively service. Carol was instrumental in bringing issues of contemporary worship to the church. As you plan worship experiences in your class, consider the following things:

• Are the hymns you most often sing written before or after 1890?
• Is the language understandable for someone new (or long absent) coming into the church?
• Is the language inclusive (age, gender, marital status)?

Carol decided to return to work several years after joining the church, so she needed childcare after school. Some members of the church were becoming aware of the need for an after-school program in the community, but Carol was the impetus that got the church moving. With prayers and determination, the church began an after-school program for the community. School buses pull up each afternoon and drop off about twenty children, who now do not have to go into an empty house with no one to greet them. The church is serving the community by meeting a need and providing a safe and caring environment for children of working parents.

Carol and Dan were reluctant to attend evening classes or participate in other small groups because they needed childcare. The church recognized that a number of families had this need, so they began providing childcare at the church for every evening event, whether educational, worship, social, or administrative.

Dan works for a large corporation and often has to make ethical decisions about corporate policy. He says it is sometimes hard to stand up for what he believes in the face of the corporate culture and meeting the bottom line. He has said it is his faith that carries him through the tough times from Sunday morning to Saturday night. He depends on his Sunday school class to help him struggle with how his faith affects the decisions he makes.

Dan plays the trumpet, which is a joy for him and a gift he likes to give his faith community. At the beginning of Lent several years ago, he approached the choir director with a piece of music that had a trumpet introit he wanted to play. The choir director was delighted, as were the rest of the congregation.

Carol is a gifted teacher. She has taught in the regular Sunday school program and is now co-leading the junior high youth in the church. She believes strongly in using her gift and chooses carefully where she will spend her time. Between being a wife, mother, and wage earner, she has little extra time. Therefore, she chooses activities that will use her gifts, provide excellent teaching for her children, and help her to grow in faith.

There are many spiritual gifts inventories to help class members discover their spiritual gifts and use this information to serve the church by sharing what God has given to them. (See page 86.) There also are surveys that will invite people to name their passions, but it is up to the church to discover how best to use the passions of the congregation to serve the faith community. Most people are willing to share those things they are passionate about.

Some Things to Think About

1. Think about your class. Who are the working families who have children? What are their needs? How is your class and the church helping to meet those needs?

2. Are there adults who are not able to participate in the educational ministries of the church because of a lack of childcare? If so, what steps could be taken to enable their participation?

3. Does your class provide opportunities for members to discover their spiritual gifts? Are there opportunities for those gifts to be used?

4. How does your class help members apply their faith to the issues they face every day?

Samantha

Samantha, who is known as Sam, is a career-oriented woman in her mid-twenties. She was raised in the church, but she dropped out during college and has not returned. She is living in a city away from home because of her career.

During high school Sam was part of a youth mission group that came from various United Methodist churches and traveled to different parts of the world to spread the message of God's love by interacting with other youth. It was a life-changing event for her because she experienced looking beyond her circle of friends and daily routine to serve others. Now she is searching for something more in her life. Sam dabbled in New Age spirituality, but she found it lacking in what she calls the basics. She thinks the churches she has attended are boring and do not meet her needs.

Sam is tired of the bar scene and has come to realize there is no one there with whom she wants to spend any significant time. She does not know where to go to find interesting people with values similar to hers.

Your class may include people like Sam, who are beginning careers after college and looking for ways to make a difference. Many of them got what they wanted while growing up, but they are beginning to settle down and realize that life is not all about getting. They are searching for some way to give of themselves.

Consider the following when teaching young adults:

- Many young adults may want or need a mentor. Professionals in your church might be willing to serve as mentors or coaches to help with career choices or networking and to give advice about particular fields or opportunities.

- Young adults may be looking for a place to serve. Class mission and service projects can provide a significant way for young adults to learn and make a difference in the world. Because people in this age group may be changing jobs and schedules frequently, short-term projects with a definite beginning and end are often the most successful. Most young adults want to know that the service they are engaged in really does make a difference in the lives of others. Tutoring programs, Habitat for Humanity building projects, Volunteers in Mission trips, and assisting at homeless shelters are examples of service-learning projects you may want to consider.

- Sunday mornings may not be the best time to hold a class for young adults. Look at the lives of the class members; then choose times and locations that fit their needs. Possible times may include Sunday lunch, Saturday afternoons, or weekday evenings.

Some Things to Think About

1. Who are the young adults in your community? What are they doing? Where do they hang out? What do they do for fun? What are their goals? How might the church fit into their lives?

2. What are the current learning opportunities for young adults in your congregation?

3. What are the opportunities for young adults to be in service in your congregation?

4. What are the opportunities for mentoring in your class? How could mentoring relationships be established?

Fred and Ruth

Fred and Ruth are in their early eighties, and the church has always been a central focus in their lives. They come to every Bible study class the church offers and hold the wisdom of the ages.

Fred and Ruth are trying to make sense of the issues they face as aging adults. Over the last few years, many of their lifelong friends have died. They look to their faith to help them deal with the loss. Fred loves to talk about and tell stories from the Bible. Many older adults have such wisdom to tell about life and faith and about how the two interconnect.

Many older adults are hungry for Bible study. Because of their more-flexible (but not necessarily less-busy) schedules, you may consider some of these suggestions:

- A daytime Bible study such as DISCIPLE, which is a thirty-four-week comprehensive study of the Bible, meets the needs of people who would like to spend in-depth time working with Scripture and sharing their faith with others.
- A weekday luncheon Bible study on the Scripture that will be preached on the following Sunday is an interesting way to prepare for worship. If your church uses the Common Lectionary (specific Scriptures that are used interdenominationally and internationally for each Sunday), ask for a copy of a calendar that has the Scriptures listed. If your pastor does not use the Lectionary, ask for the Scripture ahead of time.
- Many adults like to have a Monday-morning quarterback session over coffee and muffins to discuss the Scripture and sermon from the previous day.
- Neighborhood Bible study groups provide a cozy atmosphere and shorter travel distances. People can meet in alternating homes or in a home that is centrally located in a neighborhood or that has the most room and accessibility. Food is always a drawing card.
- Interfaith Bible study groups provide a means of exchanging ideas and beliefs in a loving atmosphere. Making discoveries about how others view God is usually fascinating and pulls us to take a deeper look at our faith foundation.

Fred and Ruth like to feel needed in the faith community. One of the greatest human needs is the desire to feel needed. Often, seniors begin to feel they are no longer needed. The church seems to be functioning with younger, brighter faces, which makes seniors feel as if they have been put out to pasture. Fred is a regular participant in the church's Bagel and Basics Club. Any older adult who is available comes to the church around nine on Friday mornings for coffee, bagels, and fellowship and then works with the others for an hour or so doing all the little things around the church that may fall through the cracks: dusting, polishing, making small repairs, and doing touch-up painting. Everyone wins! The church glistens and gleams, and the older adults have a social time and feel they are contributing to the good of the faith community. They take pride in the added touches that make everyone pleased with the way the church looks for members and visitors alike.

Fred and Ruth's three adult children live in other states. They keep in contact with them and the grandchildren through the phone and e-mail, but they see them only a few times a year. A few years ago when the church introduced a grandparenting program, Fred and Ruth signed up right away. They were matched with the Smith family, who live several hundred miles away from their own extended family. The Smith family includes children who are about the age of Fred and Ruth's own grandchildren. It is hard to tell who gets the most out of the relationship—Fred and Ruth or the Smiths. Fred and Ruth believe their relationship with the Smith children has helped them keep in better touch with their own grandchildren. The Smiths feel equally blessed.

Older adults have many gifts. Many are retired from professions and have skills that can be passed on, such as starting a business, financial planning, training and development, gardening, and canning. The willingness of the generations to share and learn together makes it so exciting. In the conversation that occurs during this type of interchange, faith stories, values, and Christian ethics may evolve in a natural and easy manner. Retired teachers or adults with interest in math, science, or other subjects may help children and youth who need one-on-one tutoring. Children with special needs may benefit greatly from the individual attention and caring that is expressed. In our technological age, reading stories is becoming a lost art. What fun it is for a senior to tell favorite stories and make them come alive for a child. (Just as with any church activity, remember to adhere to your church's policies and procedures for reducing the risk of child abuse.)

Fred and Ruth enjoy getting out for lunch and fellowship and going to church for dinners and work projects, so that they can be with their friends. They are active participants in the church's older adult fellowship group, which has created the Restaurant-of-the-Month Club. They frequently get a price discount because they go at off-peak times. The group also plans regular day trips to concerts, museums, movies, and other activities. Sometimes the group uses the church van; at other times they car-pool. The members of the group are intentional in making sure those who need transportation have a ride. The activities the group schedules are usually inexpensive, because many of the group's members are on fixed incomes.

Fred and Ruth enjoy learning. Since retirement they have explored many areas of interest that they did not have time for earlier in life. Ruth has discovered an interest in investing, and Fred is taking Spanish classes.

A myth of aging is that our brains slow down, making it hard to learn new things. This is indeed a myth. As our country's population continues to age, we are making discoveries and debunking myths about aging and our capabilities. Many older adults are interested in keeping up with their education. Contact your local university, community college, or even the high school to discover people available (and affordable) to lead short-term studies or seminars. Members of your congregation, or people members know, may have expertise they are willing to share.

As Fred and Ruth age, they find it more difficult to climb stairs and need extra time, and sometimes help, in getting around. They were thankful when the church installed an elevator that allows them to get to the sanctuary level of the church easily. They think the large-print bulletins and Sunday school curriculum are extremely helpful.

Are your classrooms accessible to aging or physically challenged people? I served a church that had a ramp out front, but there were sixteen stairs once you entered the front door. When I first brought the idea of accessibility to the administrative board, their response was, "Why? We don't have anyone here with disabilities." Of course they did not; anyone who was physically challenged could not get in! Two years and a consciousness-raising program and several thousands of dollars later, the church was fully accessible. To the church's delight, older adults began coming back. Once they discovered they could use the elevator and not be embarrassed by struggling to climb sixteen stairs, they came to worship and Sunday school again.

A month ago life took an unexpected turn. Fred and Ruth were enjoying their senior years until Fred had a stroke. Their world has changed totally. Where they were pillars of the church—giving their time and energy to special projects and causes, attending every Bible study class, and just being solid—they now need the church to help them. They are able to stay in contact with their adult Sunday school class and the congregation through a home visitation program. Someone visits them once each week to bring a worship bulletin, an audio tape of the service, and news from their Sunday school class. They also receive a copy of the curriculum the class is studying, which helps them feel connected to the class.

Some Things to Think About

1. What are the opportunities for lifelong learning in your community and congregation?

2. Are there other churches or community organizations you could partner with to provide educational opportunities for older adults?

3. List at least five ways your congregation creates opportunities for intergenerational learning.

4. What things do you do (or could you do) in your class to promote intergenerational learning?

5. What things may need to be changed in your church to make the educational opportunities more accessible for older adults?

6. What does your class do (or could it do) to maintain contact with those who are not able to attend class?

Joyce

Joyce, a widow in her late fifties, comes to church as much for the community as for the worship. She is active and goes to meetings and social gatherings, but she knows she will return to an empty house when the activity is over.

She found the members of her Sunday school class to be her biggest support when her husband, Frank, died. Immediately after he died they brought food, offered housing for out-of-town guests, and helped out in countless little ways. As the months went by, members continued to drop Joyce notes saying that they were thinking of her. A couple of class members called her on a regular basis to see how she was doing. They listened patiently as she expressed her feelings, never indicating by words or tone that she should not be feeling the way she did or that she should be getting through her grief faster. They never tried to fix her life.

The Sunday school class has a tradition of bringing donuts whenever one of them has a birthday. One member of the class brought donuts on Frank's birthday, and the class spent a good portion of the time reminiscing about Frank's contributions to the class. Joyce cried through some of the class, but she was grateful that people were not acting as if Frank had never existed. Sometimes when she least expects it, a hymn or prayer will remind her of Frank. The people in her class never seem to be uncomfortable with her tears. Often, someone will reach over and pat her hand or give her a quick hug.

The name of the Sunday school class is Couples for Christ. Before she became a widow, Joyce had never given the name a second thought. Now every time she sees the name above the classroom door, she thinks, *Do I still belong here?* She knows several single people in her age range who have joined the church but have not become part of any class. She wonders if they assume when they see the name that they will not be welcome in the class. While she still attends the class regularly, she sometimes feels out of place at its social events.

Shortly after Frank died, Joyce joined a support group for widows and widowers that meets monthly at the church and is cooperatively sponsored by her church and several other churches in the community. Through it she has met people who are having feelings and experiences that are similar to her own.

A while back a man in the church who had lost his wife decided to start a Christian singles group for adults over forty. He perceived a need and received the blessing of the church to use the church building as a meeting place for the group. He advertised in the local newspapers and set a date for the initial meeting. He met with Joyce and other single adults in the church and enlisted their support. People come from as far as forty miles away to be part of the group. They go to dinner, movies, and sports events together, either as a total group or as small groups.

Joyce says that one of the most distressing times of day is eating dinner alone, so she welcomes any opportunity to come together for a shared meal. She particularly enjoys participating in the supper club that was started by the church nurture committee. Old and new church members are mixed into groups of five or six that meet for supper at the home of one of the group members or at the church, depending on the needs of the group. Each person brings one item for the supper. The groups are formed again every three months.

Some Things to Think About

1. Think back to a recent class meeting. How does your class include or exclude others by language and traditions? Are there things you could change that would make the class more welcoming?

2. How are the particular needs of widowed and divorced people cared for in your class or congregation?

3. How does your class respond when a member of the class experiences a loss?

Knowing Your People

The stories you have just read are a sampling of the types of people you will find in your church and in your classes for adults. Use the profiles to help you focus on the people in your church and class. Single adults are found at all ages. Disability can strike anywhere. Parenting lasts for many years and brings age-related challenges. Adults have many and varied needs. You cannot be everything to everyone; however, the church can become a place for faith formation for adults of any age.

Every adult is unique, and different people will respond to events in their lives in different ways. However, there are some predictable stages of development that most adults experience. Having a knowledge of adult age-level characteristics can be extremely helpful in understanding the people in your classes.

On pages 72–73, you will find a chart that describes typical adult characteristics at various ages. As you read the chart, think about the people in your class. Test the characteristics listed against your own experience. Think about ways you have seen adults exhibit these characteristics.

On page 74, you will find a chart that lists some non-normative generational characteristics. While there are general characteristics that are descriptive of large numbers of adults, nearly everyone has some experiences and characteristics that are not typical for people in their age range. For example, a young adult becoming a widow, a middle adult retiring, or an older adult working full-time. Our non-normative generational experiences often are extremely significant and life-shaping.

Get to know the people you teach and learn with. When you listen deeply to the cares, concerns, hopes, and dreams of people and open yourself to the moving of the Holy Spirit, amazing opportunities for learning occur.

Adult Age-Level Characteristics

Young Adults	Middle Adults	Older Adults
Physical		
• Measuring time since birth • Learning preferences established • Reached physical peak	• Beginning to measure time as "time until death" • Coming to terms with mortality • Experiencing midlife physical changes	• Having losses and fearing losses • Learning ability may be affected by hearing and sight losses • Increasing healthcare needs and chronic illnesses
Social		
• Serving others versus being self-absorbed • Needing others versus being emotionally distant • Finding one's place in society and community • Struggling with independence	• Serving others versus being self-absorbed • Range of interests include career planning, personal growth, relationship development, problem solving, and values clarification	• Life has meaning versus life with regrets • Adjustment to retirement • Close relationships dwindling through death • Increasing dependence on others • Volunteerism and caregiving are important
Emotional		
• Entering adult world • Need intimacy • Settling down • Need to be accepted	• Managing mid-life transitions (death of parents, empty nest) • Shedding burdens of early childhood	• Need to be valued, accepted, and respected by people and institutions
Intellectual		
• Learn best when not under stress • Time is valuable • Prefer problem-centered learning over subject-centered learning • Want to apply learning to daily life	• Self-directed learning • Want to be involved in decisions about learning • Want input from knowledgeable people, resources, and groups	• Build on life experiences • Use visual images and mental pictures to enhance learning • Encourage self-paced and problem-centered learning activities

START HERE

Young Adults	Middle Adults	Older Adults
Spiritual		
• Many seek spiritual experiences • May be returning to church • Some want answers; others want the opportunity to raise questions and search	• Want to understand the meaning of life, values, priorities, and one's place in the world • Take responsibility for one's own spiritual needs	• Want an arena in which to grow in faith and to accept life story • Need purpose in life • Need to feel life is worth living • May want to tell one's life and faith story and mentor others
Special Needs		
• Want to be treated and respected as adults and peers • Want arenas for fellowship, service, and ministry to others	• Context, as well as the climate, of learning is important for learning and thinking • Traumatic events often cause involvement in learning activities	• Opportunities for continued growth • Significant service verses busy work • Daytime activities and accessible surroundings • Good lighting and acoustics
Gifts		
• Expanding knowledge, creativity, and intimacy • Willingness to take risks	• Dependability and steadiness • Concern for the future • Financial resources	• Wisdom • Time • Endurance • Objectivity • Life experiences • Hope • Acceptance of death
Vocation		
• Seeking fulfilling work • On-the-job training	• Questioning • Career changes • Mentoring	• Retirement from primary career • May reenter or reinvent work

Non-Normative Adult Generational Characteristics

(out-of-the-ordinary or unexpected events in adulthood)

Young Adult	Middle Adult	Older Adult
Relationship		
• Widowhood	• Married once and still married	• First Divorce
Family		
• Caring for aging parents	• Having no children	• Raising grandchildren
• Death of parent	• Death of child	• Death of grandchild
Social		
• Home owner	• Retired	• Working full-time
• Debt-free		
Spiritual		
• Biblically literate	• Regular church involvement	• Biblically illiterate
Physical		
• Rheumatoid arthritis	• Alzheimer's disease	• 20/20 vision without corrective lens

Some Things to Think About

1. As you think about young adults you know, what other characteristics would you add to these charts? for middle adults? for older adults?

2. In what stage of life are most of your students? What are the events that have shaped their lives?

3. Think about the people in your class. What out-of-the-ordinary or unexpected events have occurred in their lives? How have these events shaped their lives?

4. Think about yourself. What historic event has had the most effect on your life? What unexpected events have you experienced?

5. How do the life events and age-level characteristics of your students influence the way you teach?

Section Three
Now What?

The Future

What does the future of adult Christian education look like? The honest answer is, "I do not know." However, I do have some strong indications of what things will look like for making disciples of adults as they travel their journey of faith.

I believe that people are more important than programs, and that it is essential to take time to know your students beyond a surface level. Discover their dreams and fears, their doubts and questions, their heart's desire. Let them know they are important to you, and convince them they are important to God. The faith community needs to be a place where people are known and loved for who they are, warts and all. Create a climate of love and acceptance.

Disciples must become witnesses in word and deed. Encourage your students to walk their talk. We cannot be just hearers of the Word; we also must be doers of the Word. Adults need to be involved in making a difference in their world.

Forming a Vision and Mission

Effective educational ministries for adults require a vision for ministry. Adult teachers can be leaders in helping the church develop a mission and vision. Without direction, the faithful will falter. If we are to continue as a faith-building community, we must have a common vision and mission that points us to the future in a faith-forming way and helps us create learning and serving opportunities for adults that will help the vision become a reality.

As you work to establish your own vision for adult ministry, remember that adults need

- places they can witness to their faith;
- ways to live out their faith in daily life;
- ways to continually grow in their understanding of Scripture;
- settings where they can be accountable for their growth in discipleship;
- opportunities to wrestle with their most profound hopes, fears, desires, and questions.

As you create learning and serving opportunities to make the vision become a reality, consider ways you can
- translate informational learning to formational learning;
- develop a plan to feed the spiritual hunger of adults;
- use existing and developing technology in both informational and formational ways;
- provide time for adults to hear the stories of others and to tell their own stories, interpreting them in the light of the gospel;
- use all intelligences in teaching and preaching;
- provide small-group interaction;
- provide means for adults to rediscover the Bible;
- provide ways to put faith into action;
- teach and model transformational love rather than judgment and condemnation.

Teaching for Transformation

Teaching and learning with adults is not a linear, step-by-step process. The items previously mentioned work to complement and reinforce one another. When you encourage transformation, you put faith into action. When you seek ways to fill the spiritual hunger of adults, you find yourself telling and hearing faith stories, rediscovering the Bible, and using all of the different ways that people learn.

Information is necessary, for we cannot act out of ignorance. We need to be informed before we can be formed. We need to explore and understand the foundational stories of the Bible. We need to make connections between the biblical story and our own lives. We must be aware of the relationship between God and God's people from the beginning through the present time.

But if we stop there, we are doing everyone—God, ourselves, and our students—a disservice. Just to know the story as a cognitive task is not enough, for it is only half the task of this ministry. We need to guide and encourage adult students to take the next and imperative step of using that information to change their lives. They must be informed to be transformed. Adults have a spiritual hunger that must be filled.

A walk down the self-help aisle of any bookstore confirms this hunger. Adults are asking whether that is all there is and are searching for answers. The same bookstore has aisles of New Age and other alternative spirituality books that are guaranteed to fill the spiritual void in our lives.

We have a better answer. The simple but profound answer is God. We do not have to search the universe for a higher power. We do not have to follow our bliss. We have God and God's teachings through the incarnate word of God's Son to show us the way. We must discover ways to make our teachings as exciting and attractive as are the alternative messages.

That spiritual hunger is fed both in the words of Scripture and in the way we live our lives based on Scripture. There is no greater high than living God's way. When we are informed and transformed, we discover the peace that passes understanding, and it changes everything we do, say, think, or feel.

Living in an Increasingly High-tech World

More and more adults have never known a world without TV, and they cannot imagine how they got along without computers or cell phones. The church must use this technology or be left in the ever-increasing dust.

My church uses the Internet and e-mail to keep the congregation informed of activities and prayer requests. Visitors and new residents can find churches through the Internet. We are aware that this technology will not go away and that people's lives are more and more connected through the Internet. Therefore, to tap into their habits and ways they stay informed, we must provide this connection.

Some churches are using computer-based training to engage students in Bible study. Videos play an increasingly important role in our visually oriented society. Adult students no longer have to rely on pictures in books to get visual images of life in Jesus' time or to see what is happening in the Mediterranean world today. With the flip of a switch, they can see it in living color.

Adults today are oriented to a fast-paced information-laden world. Churches that do not keep up are labeled as old-fashioned, or worse. As we increase our use of technology, we must not neglect the importance of human interactions and relationships. Sometimes this is referred to as balancing high-tech and high-touch.

The secular world often offers high-tech more effectively than the church can, but the church can provide balance by offering a high-touch environment in which feelings are freely expressed. When we talk about the joys we want to celebrate or concerns that weigh heavy on our hearts, we are connected to our faith community in critical ways. We need to tell our stories and share our laughter and tears with real people, not with machines.

In my church we hold the hand of someone near us as the pastoral prayer and Lord's Prayer are said. It is a visual and tactile connection that is symbolic of our connection to God. For some, it is the only time they are touched during the week. Touching another human (in appropriate places and ways) is a basic human need. The church needs to provide the balance of high-touch.

Telling Our Stories

Adult's lives are sometimes so busy and controlled that they do not have the time or the place to calm down and get in touch with who and whose they are. We can provide the time and place to connect.

Adults have stories, and they need an opportunity to tell those stores and to make the connection of how their stories connect with God's story. Faith happens in those intersections. As it was from the beginning of time, our history is in our stories. Each time people tell their story, they relive it and revive their faith; therefore, storytelling is an important factor in faith development.

Even adults who are new to the church or to faith have stories. They need to be encouraged to tell why, where, when, and how they came to be part of this particular adult group. Adults need to hear the stories of others.

As adults who are new to faith or pillars of the faith listen to the stories of others, they can make the connections of how God is at work in the lives of others. Telling our story and having someone listen is a critical part of well-being and growth.

Adults must be taught how to listen. Strange but true. Most adults have learned how to read, to write, and to speak; but seldom are they taught to listen. Listening is an active task. It means closing down your "background conversation," or thinking about what you are going to say in reply. Listening involves your whole body, not just your ears. Good listeners maintain eye contact, lean slightly forward, keep focused, and avoid distractions. Listening is not problem solving or one-upmanship; it is giving yourself entirely to the other person. It is a gift. When people really listen to another's story, they often learn a powerful lesson of life and faith.

Learning in Many Ways

Adults need to learn the skills of using all of their intelligences to reach their full intellectual potential. As adults are awakened to and become active in using all of their intelligences, powerful learning often takes place. Adults are constantly amazed at what they are capable of when they tap into an underused intelligence. In training events, adults often either will applaud or sit in awe of a profound statement made by someone in the class. Even the adult who has written the words, dramatized the role, or sung the song is amazed at what he or she has produced.

We all have the potential. As adults, we often do not use all of our ways of knowing. When we activate those intelligences, we gain access to ways of understanding that often provide profound insight.

Interacting in Small-Groups

Small groups are not just a good idea, but are critical to our well-being. We need to connect with a small group of people who genuinely care about us: our needs, fears, joys, and celebrations. We need to walk into our church and have people who know us and love us. We need to practice unconditional love and acceptance of one another. We need to know we are missed when we are not present. It is not just a psycho-social need; it is a spiritual need. Therefore, the church can provide a potentially life-saving gift by offering small-group ministry.

Rediscovering the Bible

Many adults today confess to going to church when they were children but dropping out during their college years. Some return to ensure that their children have a Christian education. Some come back to try to find that illusive something that is missing in their lives. Some come out of curiosity. Whatever the reason, adults are returning to church.

You cannot make the assumption that adults know anything about the Bible. Even adults who grew up in the church may have retained little or no information.

When you help adults to rediscover the Bible, you must be excited and enthusiastic about its life-changing potential. Our Bible is not just a story written thousands of years ago; it is a living document that is filled with exciting stories of God's continual relationship with God's people. The Bible is our book, and we will carry it into our future!

A Last Word

You must teach and model transformational love rather than judgment and condemnation. We all make mistakes! The world often ridicules, judges, confronts, and condemns us for this. When we model Jesus' love, Christ is present in our midst—healing, reconciling, and saving.

Some Things to Think About

1. What changes are occurring in your community? What effect do you think those changes will have on your congregation?

2. List what you believe are the five most important things you do as a teacher.

3. How would you describe your vision for Christian education with your class?

4. How do you think members of your class would describe the mission and vision of the class? (Ask them.)

5. Identify a transforming experience in your own faith journey. How does that experience continue to shape you?

6. Name five ways your class uses, or could use, technology to further its mission.

7. As a teacher, what are your plans for continued learning?

Posttest

When you began reading this book, you were asked to take this quiz. Now take the quiz again. Compare your answers from the earlier quiz (page 7) to the answers to this one. Have any of your ideas changed?

Write an *A* for *Agree,* a *D* for *Disagree,* or a *U* for *Undecided* beside each statement.

____ 1. The major ministry with adults is to encourage memorizing Scripture to use in times of need.

____ 2. Adults learn in a variety of ways.

____ 3. Adults need a safe environment in order to speak what is on their hearts.

____ 4. Community building is a waste of precious time with people who attend church together.

____ 5. Adults go through predictable transitions of faith development throughout their lives.

____ 6. Adult classes need to be pastor-led to have credibility.

____ 7. Adults need a structured class setting in order to learn.

____ 8. Expression of feelings has no place in an adult class.

____ 9. Many adults are searching for a meaningful faith.

____ 10. Adult classes must meet on Sunday morning to have the most impact on people's lives.

____ 11. Adults come to class with many and diverse wants and needs.

____ 12. Every adult class must have a trained teacher to be effective.

____ 13. Storytelling is for children.

____ 14. Prayer is a vital part of any adult Christian learning situation.

____ 15. Every adult class needs to stick with the chosen curriculum for the best learning to happen.

____ 16. Many adults are embarrassed by their lack of biblical knowledge.

____ 17. The Coffeepot Class (just hanging out) is an excuse for adults who do not want to learn.

____ 18. Adult classes work best when they are homogeneous in nature.

____ 19. You must have a minimum of ten adults for a class to be successful.

Additional Resources

This book is just an introduction to the many issues involved in teaching and learning with adults. As the title indicates, it is a starting point, not the final destination. As you read this book, reflected on the questions, and talked with others, you may have discovered areas where you need to gather additional information or develop new skills. The resources listed in this section will help you to take the next steps along the road of teaching and learning with adults.

Books

A Faithful Future: Teaching and Learning for Discipleship, by Carol F. Krau, Judith M. Bunyi, N. Lynne Westfield, Joyce Brown, Barbara Bruce, and Ben Marshall (Nashville: Discipleship Resources, 1999).

Aging: God's Challenge to Church and Synagogue, by Richard H. Gentzler, Jr. and Donald F. Clingan (Nashville: Discipleship Resources, 1996).

Becoming Adult, Becoming Christian: Adult Development and Christian Faith, by James W. Fowler (San Francisco: Jossey-Bass Publishers, 2000).

Discovering and Exploring Habits of Mind, edited by Arthur L. Costa and Bena Kallick (Alexandria, VA: Association for Supervision and Curriculum Development, 2000).

Emotional Intelligence: Why It Can Matter More Than IQ, by Daniel Goleman (New York: Bantam Books, 1995).

Foundations: Shaping the Ministry of Christian Education in Your Congregation (Nashville: Discipleship Resources, 1993).

Frames of Mind: The Theory of Multiple Intelligences (Second Edition), by Howard Gardner (New York: Basic Books, 1993).

Intelligence Reframed: Multiple Intelligences for the 21st Century, by Howard Gardner (New York: Basic Books, 1999).

Keeping in Touch: Christian Formation and Teaching, by Carol F. Krau (Nashville: Discipleship Resources, 1999).

Learning to Lead From Your Spiritual Center, by Patricia D. Brown (Nashville: Abingdon Press, 1996).

Mapping the Mind, by Rita Carter (Berkeley, CA: University of California Press, 1998).

Planning for Christian Education: A Practical Guide for Your Congregation, edited by Carol Fouts Krau (Nashville: Discipleship Resources, 1994).

Postmoderns: The Beliefs, Hopes, and Fears of Young Americans (1965–1981), by Craig Kennet Miller (Nashville: Discipleship Resources, 1996).

Quest: A Journey Toward a New Kind of Church, by Dan R. Dick with Evelyn M. Burry (Nashville: Discipleship Resources, 1999).

7 Ways of Teaching the Bible to Adults: Using Our Multiple Intelligences to Build Faith, by Barbara Bruce (Nashville: Abingdon Press, 2000).

Teaching the Bible to Adults and Youth, by Dick Murray (Nashville: Abingdon Press, rev. 1993).

Teaching With the Brain in Mind, by Eric Jensen (Alexandria, VA: Association for Supervision and Curriculum Development, 1998).

The MI Strategy Banks, by Ellen Arnold (Tucson: Zephyr Press, 1998).

The Mozart Effect: Tapping the Power of Music to Heal the Body, Strengthen the Mind, and Unlock the Creative Spirit, by Don Campbell (New York: Avon Books, 1997).

Web Sites

http://www.discipleshipresources.org
    Additional copies of this book as well as other resources can be ordered through this Discipleship Resources online bookstore.

http://www.gbod.org/adult
    This site, which is sponsored by the General Board of Discipleship of The United Methodist Church, includes articles, event information, newsletters, and other links related to adult ministries.

http://www.gbod.org/education
    This site, which is sponsored by the General Board of Discipleship of The United Methodist Church, includes articles, event information, newsletters, and other links related to education.

http://www.newhorizons.org

This site includes articles that are written by experts about the latest hot topics in education.

http://pzweb.harvard.edu

Project Zero is an educational research group at the Harvard Graduate School of Education. Their mission is to understand and enhance learning, thinking, and creativity in the arts, as well as in humanistic and scientific disciplines, at individual and institutional levels.

http://zephyrpress.com/articles.htm

This site, which is sponsored by Zephyr Press, has a variety of articles on multiple intelligences and other educational theories.

http://www.osiem.org/ospre/enhanced/creativity.htm

This site has more information about Barbara Bruce, the author of *Start Here*.

For more information on recommended resources for gifts discernment, contact: Office of Stewardship Ministries, General Board of Discipleship, P.O. Box 340003, Nashville, TN 37203-0003. Phone: 877-899-2780.